PEGASUS ENCYCLOPEDIA LIBRARY

Space
STARS

Edited by: Pallabi B. Tomar, Hitesh Iplani
Managing editor: Tapasi De
Designed by: Vijesh Chahal, Anil Kumar, Rohit Kumar
Illustrated by: Suman S. Roy, Tanoy Choudhury
Colouring done by: Vinay Kumar, Kiran Kumari & Pradeep Kumar

CONTENTS

Introduction 3

Evolution of stars 5

What are stars made of? 9

Characteristics of stars 11

Types of stars 13

Twinkling of stars 17

The colour of stars 19

Naming stars 21

Distribution of stars 22

Classification of stars 24

Studying and watching stars 27

Some brightest stars 29

Test Your Memory 31

Index 32

Introduction

For thousands of years, human beings have looked at the night sky and wondered about the things they saw. Ancient people believed they could see shapes among the stars. They identified both animals and people and each had its own story. These chance alignments of the stars are known as **constellations**. Today, 88 constellations are used by astronomers to organize the night sky and to identify the locations of the stars. Stars are the most plentiful objects in the visible universe. They provide the light and energy that fuels a solar system. They also create the heavy elements that are necessary to form life. Without stars, there would be no life. The sun provides energy for nearly every living thing on Earth. It also warms our planet's surface to create a virtual oasis in the coldness of space.

Astonishing fact

Double stars are two stars that look like one to the naked eye but separate in a telescope view.

What is a star?

A star is a huge, shining ball in space that produces a tremendous amount of light and other forms of energy. The sun is a star, and it supplies Earth with light and heat energy. The stars look like twinkling points of light except for the sun. The sun looks like a ball because it is much closer to Earth than any other star.

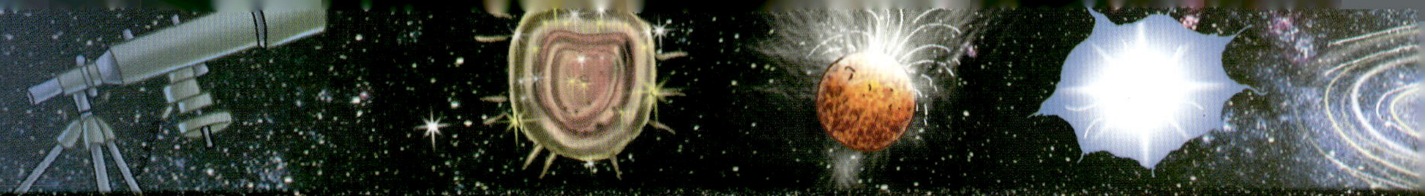

STARS

To many people, a star is simply one of many bright glowing lights in the sky at night. In reality, stars are much more complex. A star is actually a self-luminous celestial body consisting of a mass of gas that is held together by its own gravity. The glowing light typically seen from Earth is caused by actual nuclear reactions occurring within the stars core. These nuclear reactions are balanced by the outflow of energy to the surface of the star which produces the glow we so commonly associate with stars here on Earth.

Stars are cosmic energy engines that produce heat, light, ultraviolet rays, x-rays, and other forms of radiation. They are composed largely of gas and plasma, a superheated state of matter composed of subatomic particles.

No one knows how many stars exist, but the number would be staggering. Our universe likely contains more than 100 billion galaxies and each of those galaxies may have more than 100 billion stars!

Astonishing fact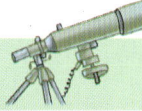

When an average-sized star dies, it sheds its outer layers, which causes the formation of planetary nebula. The Cat's Eye Nebula is the best example of a planetary nebula.

Evolution of stars

It is common knowledge, that a bright star is also the hottest one and the small or dim ones are the coolest stars. Depending on this primary hypothesis, a star is studied for further information about its origin. Stars like **Vega** are a huge mass of cold and dusty clouds made up of gases. The gravitational force causes the gases to contract. The assembling of matter in close formations leads to a rise in temperature. This rise in temperature leads to a chain of nuclear reactions in the atoms of the components present. The reason why we see luminous bodies in space is because of the energy released during chemical reactions in the stellar area.

The dusty mass consists of a large amount of hydrogen. The nucleus of a hydrogen atom undergoes a nuclear fusion reaction, to transform into helium. This conversion is accompanied by a steady release of a huge amount of energy. This is visible as a radiant light in space. This sequence of events lasts for about 10 billion years in the case of an average or medium sized star. For instance, the sun (which is a medium sized star) is believed to be 5 billion years old and may live on for another 5 billion years!

Astonishing fact

The constellation of Cygnus (Swan) contains the very biggest star in the known universe—a hyper giant which is almost a million times as big as the sun!

STARS

Stars form when cool, relatively dense clouds (molecular clouds) of interstellar gas and dust shrink upon themselves as a result of gravitational collapse. In a spiral galaxy such as the Milky Way, star formation is usually triggered when gas clouds are compressed by shock waves.

The birthplace of stars

Stars are born in regions of unstable clouds of dust and gas which are scattered throughout the outer spiral arms of our Milky Way. Hundreds of newborn stars are nursed in the Orion Nebula, which is just visible to the naked eye as a fuzzy speck of light in the constellation of Orion. However, the lit up regions of the nebula only represent a small portion, as much of the nebula is actually full of dense molecular clouds which absorb visible light and can only be probed with radio waves.

The formation of stars

Once the clouds start to collapse, the material breaks down into massive lumps, and as these continue to collapse, gravitational compression causes the lumps of cloud to warm up as gravitational potential energy is converted into heat. It is these lumps that will eventually form a single star, two stars or even a star with its own planetary system.

As the pressure and temperature increases in these lumps, a sphere made up of superhot gas called a **proto-star** (a potential star) is formed. This proto-star will continue to collapse until its core approaches close to 10 million Kelvin's as that is the required temperature to undergo nuclear fusion.

Astonishing fact

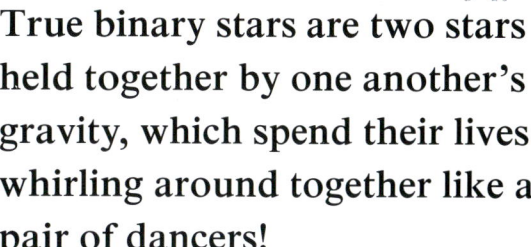

True binary stars are two stars held together by one another's gravity, which spend their lives whirling around together like a pair of dancers!

The entire formation process of a star like our sun, might take about 50 million years. Once a star has begun the conversion of hydrogen into helium, the remainder of its life will be determined exclusively by its mass. This nuclear reaction releases heat and produces an outward pressure which supports and holds up the star against further gravitational collapse for as long as there is enough nuclear fuel to burn.

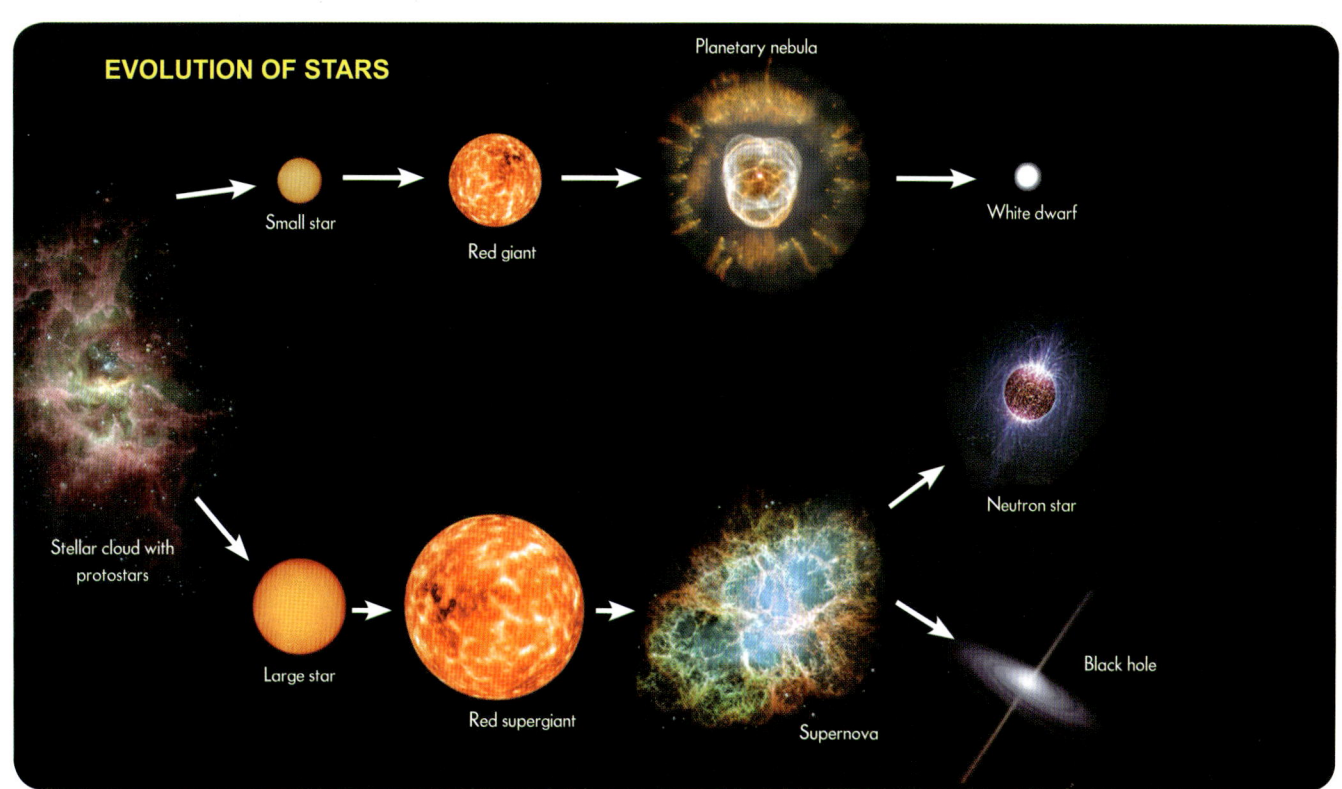

STARS

The end of an era

After exhausting all readily available hydrogen in its core, nuclear fusion comes to a halt and the core begins to contract due to gravity. Stars with masses between 0.5 and 8 solar masses (1 solar mass is the mass of the sun) expand to become **red giants**.

These massive stars have a radius several hundred times the size of our sun and each will ultimately expel its outer shell. The expelled material is called a **planetary nebula** as it resembles a giant planet when observed through an optical telescope. This ring of expelled material will remain visible for about 10 thousand years before gradually dispersing into interstellar space. The star is now dead as it has no fuel. All that is left is a **white dwarf star**.

A violent death

The evolution of stars with masses greater than 8 solar masses is not as pleasant but much more dramatic. As a result of their sheer size, these stars burn through their hydrogen supply at a faster rate but at the cost of a considerably shortened lifespan. Once their hydrogen to helium conversion phase is over, they expand to become red **supergiants**.

These are the largest stars in existence in terms of radii. Once, all its energy is spent, the red supergiant collapses and explodes as a **supernova**, shining briefly with the light of a billion suns. Most of this material is expelled into space. All that remains is a spherical body of incredible density which will either collapse into a **neutron star** or possibly, a **black hole**.

Astonishing fact

The sun is about 5 billion years old and half way through its life. As a medium sized star it will probably live for another 10 billion years.

What are stars made of?

Stars are made of the same stuff as the rest of the Universe: 73 per cent hydrogen, 25 per cent helium, and the last 2 per cent are all the other elements.

After the Big Bang, 13.7 billion years ago, the entire Universe was a hot dense sphere. The conditions inside this young Universe were so hot that it was equivalent to being inside the core of a star. In other words, the entire Universe was like a star. And for the brief time that the Universe was in this state, nuclear fusion reactions converted hydrogen into helium to the ratios we see today.

The Universe kept expanding and cooling down, and eventually the hydrogen and helium cooled down to the point that it could actually start collecting together with its mutual gravity. This is how the first stars were born. And just like the stars we have today, they were made up of roughly 73 per cent hydrogen and 25 per cent helium. These first stars were enormous and probably detonated as supernova within a million years of forming. In their life, and in their death, these first stars created some of the heavier elements that we have here on Earth, like oxygen, carbon, gold and uranium.

Astonishing fact

The brightest stars in the night sky are not actually stars, but the planets Jupiter, Venus, Mars and Mercury.

STARS

Astonishing fact

The most massive stars can be as much as 3 billion km away (our sun is only 1384, 03 km across). If one such massive star were in the solar system, it would gobble up 6 planets, including our Earth!

Stars have been forming since the Universe began. In fact, astronomers calculate that 5 new stars form in the Milky Way every year. Some have more of the heavier elements left over from previous stars; these are metal-rich stars. Others have less of these elements; the metal-poor stars. But even so, the ratio of elements is still roughly the same. Our own sun is an example of a metal rich star with a higher than average amount of heavier elements inside it. And yet, the sun's ratios are very similar; 71 per cent hydrogen, 27.1 per cent helium, and then the rest as heavier elements, like oxygen, carbon, nitrogen, etc. Of course, the sun has been converting hydrogen into helium in its core for 4.5 billion years.

Stars everywhere are made of the same stuff—3/4 hydrogen and 1/4 helium. It's the stuff left over from the formation of the universe and one of the most elegant pieces of evidence to help explain how we are here today.

Characteristics of stars

A star is a massive ball of plasma that emits light throughout the universe. A star can be defined by five basic characteristics— brightness, colour, surface temperature, size and mass.

Brightness

Two characteristics define brightness— **luminosity** and **magnitude.** Luminosity is the amount of light that a star radiates. The size of the star and its surface temperature determines its luminosity. Apparent magnitude of a star is its visible brightness, factoring in size and distance, while absolute magnitude is its true brightness irrespective of its distance from Earth.

Colour

A star's colour depends on its surface temperature. Cooler stars tend to be redder in colour, while hotter stars have a bluer appearance. Stars in the mid ranges are white or yellow such as our sun. Stars can also blend colours, such as red-orange stars or blue-white stars.

Astonishing fact

Betelgeuse, the bright star on Orion's top-left shoulder, is so big that if it was placed where the sun is, it would swallow up Earth, Mars and Jupiter!

STARS

Astonishing fact

It's estimated that the number of stars in the universe is greater than the number of grains of sand on all the beaches in the world!

Surface temperature

Astronomers measure a star's temperature on the Kelvin scale (K). Zero degree on the Kelvin scale is equal to -273.15 degrees Celsius. The coolest, reddest stars are approximately 2,500 K, while the hottest stars can reach upto 50,000 K. Our sun is about 5,500 K.

Size

Astronomers measure the size of a given star in terms of our own sun's radius. Thus, a star that measure 1 solar radii would be the same size as our sun. The star Rigel, which is much larger than our sun, measures 78 solar radii. A star's size, along with its surface temperature determines its luminosity.

Mass

A star's mass is also measured in terms of our own sun, with 1 equal to the size of our sun. For instance, Rigel, which is much larger than our sun, has a mass of 3.5 solar masses. Two stars of a similar size may not necessarily have the same mass, as stars can vary greatly in density.

Types of stars

Main Sequence Stars

The main sequence is the point in a star's evolution during which it maintains a stable nuclear reaction. It is this stage during which a star will spend most of its life. Our sun is a main sequence star. A **main sequence star** will experience only small fluctuations in luminosity and temperature. The amount of time a star spends in this phase depends on its mass. Large, massive stars will have a short main sequence stage while less massive stars will remain in main sequence much longer. Very massive stars will exhaust their fuel in only a few hundred million years. Smaller stars, like the sun, will burn for several billion years during their main sequence stage. Very massive stars will become blue giants during their main sequence.

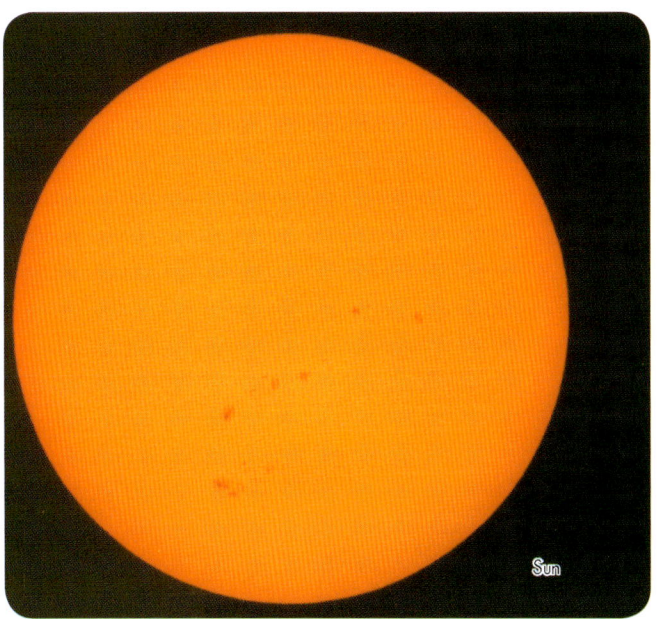

Red Giant Stars

Red Giant Stars

A **red giant** is a large star that is reddish or orange in colour. It represents the late phase of development in a star's life, when its supply of hydrogen has been exhausted and helium is being fused. This causes the star to collapse, raising the temperature in the core. The outer surface of the star expands and cools, giving it a reddish colour. Red giants are very large, reaching sizes of over 100 times the star's original size.

Astonishing fact

Our galaxy has approximately 250 billion stars and it is estimated by astronomers that there are 100 billion other galaxies in the universe!

White Dwarf Stars

A **white dwarf** is the remnant of an average-sized star that has passed through the red giant stage of its life after the star has used up its remaining fuel. At this point the star may expel some of its matter into space, creating a planetary nebula. What remains is the dead core of the star. Nuclear fusion no longer takes place. The core glows because of its residual heat. Eventually the core will radiate all of its heat into space and cool down to become what is known as a black dwarf. White dwarf stars are very dense. Their size is about the same as that of the Earth, but they contain as much mass as the sun. They are extremely hot, reaching temperatures of over 100,000 degrees!

Blue Giant Stars

Blue giants blaze with a surface temperature of 20,000 K or more and are extremely luminous. Just for comparison, a star like our sun only has a surface temperature of about 6,000 K. A blue giant star can emit 10,000 times as much energy as the sun.

As the blue stars are large and compact, they burn their fuel quickly, which gives them a very high temperature. These stars often run out of fuel in only 10,000-100,000 years.

White dwarf stars

All of the stars comprising the Milky Way galaxy revolve around the centre of the galaxy once every 200 million years or so.

Types of stars

Variable Stars

A **variable star** is a star that changes in brightness. These fluctuations can range from seconds to years depending on the type of variable star. Stars usually change their brightness when they are young and when they are old and dying. They are classified as either intrinsic or extrinsic. Intrinsic variables change their brightness because of conditions within the stars themselves. Extrinsic variables change brightness because of some external factor, like an orbiting companion star. These are also known as eclipsing binaries.

Binary Stars

Many stars in the universe are part of a multiple star system. A **binary star** is a system of two stars that are gravitationally bound to each other. They orbit around a common point, called the centre of mass. It is estimated that about half of all the stars in our galaxy are part of a binary system.

Binary stars

Variable stars

Astonishing fact

The oldest star yet discovered is HE which is 13.2 billion years old!

Red Dwarf Stars

Red dwarf stars are the most common kind of stars in the Universe. These are main sequence stars but they have such low mass that they're much cooler than stars like our sun. They have another advantage. Red dwarf stars are able to keep the hydrogen fuel mixing into their core, and so they can conserve their fuel for much longer than other stars. Astronomers estimate that some red dwarf stars will burn for up to 10 trillion years. The smallest red dwarfs are 0.075 times the mass of the sun, and they can have a mass of up to half of the sun.

Neutron stars

Neutron Stars

If a star has between 1.35 and 2.1 times the mass of the sun, it doesn't form a white dwarf when it dies. Instead, the star dies in a catastrophic supernova explosion, and the remaining core becomes a neutron star. As its name implies, a neutron star is an exotic type of star that is composed entirely of neutrons. This is because the intense gravity of the neutron star crushes protons and electrons together to form neutrons. If stars are even more massive, they will become black holes instead of neutron stars after the supernova goes off.

Supergiant stars

Supergiant Stars

The largest stars in the Universe are **supergiant stars**. These are monsters with dozens of times the mass of the sun. Unlike a relatively stable star like the sun, supergiants consume hydrogen fuel at an enormous rate and will consume all the fuel in their cores within just a few million years. Supergiant stars live fast and die young, detonating as supernova; completely disintegrating themselves in the process.

Astonishing fact

Some stars are 600,000 times as bright as our sun!

Twinkling of stars

If you look at the stars on a clear night, you will notice that they seem to twinkle and that they differ greatly in brightness. A much slower movement also takes place in the night sky. If you map the location of several stars for a few hours, you will observe that all the stars revolve slowly about a single point in the sky.

Twinkling of stars is caused by movements in Earth's atmosphere. Starlight enters the atmosphere as straight rays. Twinkling occurs because air movements constantly change the path of the light as it comes through the air.

How bright a star looks when viewed from Earth depends on two factors—the actual brightness of the star and the distance of the star from the Earth.

A nearby star that is actually dim can appear brighter than a distant star that is really extremely brilliant. For example, Alpha Centauri A seems to be slightly brighter than a star known as Rigel. But Alpha Centauri A emits only 1/100,000 as much light energy as Rigel. Alpha Centauri A seems brighter because it is only 1/325 as far from Earth as Rigel is - 4.4 light-years for Alpha Centauri A, 1,400 light-years for Rigel.

STARS

Polaris or the North Star is the only star in the sky that doesn't appear to move from night to night.

The scientific name for the twinkling of stars is stellar scintillation (or astronomical scintillation). Stars twinkle when we see them from the Earth's surface because we are viewing them through thick layers of turbulent (moving) air in the Earth's atmosphere.

Stars (except for the sun) appear as tiny dots in the sky. As their light travels through the many layers of the Earth's atmosphere, the light of the star is bent (refracted) many times and in random directions (light is bent when it hits a change in density like a pocket of cold air or hot air). This random refraction results in the star winking out (it looks as though the star moves a bit, and our eye interprets this as twinkling).

Stars closer to the horizon appear to twinkle more than stars that are overhead. This is because the light of stars near the horizon has to travel through more air than the light of stars overhead and so is subject to more refraction. Also, planets do not usually twinkle, because they are so close to us; they appear big enough that the twinkling is not noticeable.

The colour of stars

The colour of a star depends on its surface temperature. Our sun's surface temperature is about 6,000 K. Although it looks yellow from here on Earth, the light of the sun would actually look very white from space. This white light coming off the sun is because its temperature is 6,000 K. If the sun were cooler, it would give off light more on the red end of the spectrum and if the sun were hotter, it would look bluer.

And that's just what we see with other stars. The coolest stars in the universe are the red dwarf stars. These are stars with just a fraction of the mass of our sun (as low as 7.5% the mass of the sun). They don't burn as hot in their cores, and their surface temperature is about 3,500 K. The light released from their surface looks mostly red to our eyes (although there are different colours mixed up in there too though red is the majority).

Astonishing fact

Shooting stars are stars that collide with Earth as it moves around the sun. They heat up, glow and then burn down. It's common to see one every 15 minutes but they often move so quickly through the air that if you blink, you'll miss them!

STARS

The different colours of the stars are white, red, yellow and blue. The colour of a star determines the temperature of the surface of the star. You need to know that a star emits light in various colours of wavelengths of the electromagnetic spectrum. The surface temperature of a star determines the wavelength of the star. If the surface temperature is around 3,000 K degrees, then the colour of the star is red and if it is orange then the surface temperature is 4,000 K degrees. The colour of a star is yellow when the surface temperature is 6,000 K degrees. When the surface temperature is above 8,000 K degrees, the colour emitted appears white and if the temperature ranges between 20,000 K to 50,000 K degrees, then it is blue.

The wavelengths of blue coloured stars are short and it is an indication that these stars have higher surface temperature. The colours such as red, orange and yellow have longer wavelengths of light indicating that the star's surface temperature is low. The astronomers can determine the surface temperature of the stars by looking at the colours.

Astonishing fact

Of the billions and billions of stars in the universe, only about 6,000 can be seen from the Earth without a telescope.

Naming stars

Ancient people saw that certain stars are arranged in patterns shaped somewhat like human beings, animals or common objects. Some of these patterns called constellations came to represent figures of mythological characters. For example, the constellation Orion (the Hunter) is named after a hero in Greek mythology.

Today, astronomers use constellations, some of which were described by the ancients, in the scientific names of stars. The International Astronomical Union (IAU), the world authority for assigning names to celestial objects, officially recognizes 88 constellations. These constellations cover the entire sky. In most cases, the brightest star in a given constellation has alpha (the first letter of the Greek alphabet) as part of its scientific name.

The second brightest star in a constellation is usually designated beta, the second letter of the Greek alphabet; the third brightest is gamma and so on. The assignment of Greek letters to stars continues until all the Greek letters are used.

But the number of known stars has become so large that the IAU uses a different systems for newly discovered stars. Most new names consist of an abbreviation followed by a group of symbols. The abbreviation stands for either the type of star or a catalog that lists information about the star. For example, PSR J1302-6350 is a type of star known as a pulsar; hence the PSR in its name. The symbols indicate the star's location in the sky. The 1302 and the 6350 are coordinates that are similar to the longitude and latitude designations used to indicate locations on Earth's surface. The J indicates that a coordinate system known as J2000 is being used.

The human eye can detect only a very narrow range of light wavelengths, but stars emit non-visible light as well. And this light can help astronomers determine if 'starlight' actually comes from a star or another celestial body.

Distribution of stars

Stars are often found in huge groups called **clusters**. There are two types of clusters, open and globular.

Open clusters have mostly young, bright, blue stars that were born together. They usually have irregular shapes. The most famous open cluster is the **Pleiades**.

At 400 light years away, the Pleiades are the Earth's closest open cluster. You can see the Pleiades without a telescope.

Globular clusters can have as many as a million stars more than open clusters. They tend to have a sphere-like shape, with many stars at the centre. There are 160 globular clusters within the Milky Way. A globular cluster named M15 is the closest of its kind to Earth.

Globular clusters orbit the centre of the Milky Way in a region known as the **galactic halo.** Stars in globular clusters in the galactic halo are the oldest structures in our galaxy. Studying them has helped scientists figure out the age of the galaxy.

A massive star has a shorter lifetime than a less massive star.

Distribution of stars

Medieval Islamic astronomers gave Arabic names to many stars that are still used today, and they invented numerous astronomical instruments that could compute the positions of the stars.

Certain stars appear to move in shapes and patterns across the night sky. These patterns are constellations. Some look like animals, humans or objects. Constellations seem to travel in the sky from east to west every night, but they are really not moving. The Earth is moving, rotating on its axis. Constellations also seem to change with the seasons. Again, they are really not changing. They just look that way because Earth is revolving around the sun.

Stars are not spread uniformly across the universe, but are normally grouped into galaxies along with interstellar gas and dust. A typical galaxy contains hundreds of billions of stars, and there are more than 100 billion (10^{11}) galaxies in the observable universe. While it is often believed that stars only exist within galaxies, intergalactic stars have been discovered. Astronomers estimate that there are at least 70 sextillion (7×10^{22}) stars in the observable universe! A 2010 estimate revises the star count upward to 300 sextillion (3×10^{23})!

Astonishing fact

Some of the stars in the sky are so far that the light from them takes million of years to reach us.

Stars

Classification of stars

Stars have many sizes, ages and temperatures. Most stars do not stay in the same class for their entire life. As a star evolves, it's fuel changes and as a result, its average surface temperature and its size changes. Most stars are mainly sequence stars. These are the medium mass stars. They progress through similar stages as they evolve.

Spectral classification

The most widely used system of classification is spectral classification. Stars radiate light at different frequencies. As nuclear fusion occurs within a star, first hydrogen is used as fuel. The hydrogen is fused into helium, and eventually the star will begin to use helium as fuel. The helium becomes lithium, and so on, and each new, heavier fuel is used in succession. Each element radiates light in different areas of the spectrum. Since each element radiates a unique set of frequencies, this is like a signature that astrophysicists can use to understand what makes up a particular star.

> William Herschel was the first astronomer to attempt to determine the distribution of stars in the sky.

Classification of stars

Astronomers classify stars by colour using a series of letters: O, B, A, F, G, K and M. Under this classification, O stars are the hottest and M stars are the coolest, with the other letters coming in between. O stars are 'blue', A stars are 'white', G stars are 'yellow' and M stars are 'red'.

Since that doesn't provide enough detail, astronomers put a second number after the letter to distinguish where on G, for example, a star like our sun should be positioned. Each number is a further 10 per cent towards the next spectral letter. For example, our sun is classified as a G2 star. This means it's 20 per cent along the way towards an orange main sequence star.

Astronomers use another roman numeral at the end of the spectral letter to define the size and luminosity of a star. They range from I supergiants to V dwarfs, or main sequence stars. As our sun is a main sequence star, it would get the V designation.

So the full classification for the Sun is G2V.

Astonishing fact

Aldebaran is the brightest star in the constellation Taurus and is the 13th brightest star in the sky. It is about 40 times as big as the sun.

STARS

Hertzsprung-Russell diagram

The Hertzsprung-Russell (H-R) diagram is a graph that plots stars colour versus its luminosity. On it, astronomers plot stars' colour, temperature, luminosity, spectral type, and evolutionary stage. This represents a major step towards an understanding of stellar evolution or 'the lives of stars'.

- Most stars, including the sun, are 'main sequence stars,' fuelled by nuclear fusion converting hydrogen into helium. For these stars, the hotter they are, the brighter. These stars are in the most stable part of their existence. This stage generally lasts for about 5 billion years.

- As stars begin to die, they become giants and supergiants. These stars have depleted their hydrogen supply and are very old. The core contracts as the outer layers expand. These stars will eventually explode (becoming a planetary nebula or supernova, depending on their mass) and then become white dwarfs, neutron stars, or black holes, again depending on their mass.

- Smaller stars (like our sun) eventually become faint white dwarfs (hot, white, dim stars) that are below the main sequence. These hot, shrinking stars deplete their nuclear fuels and eventually become cold, dark, black dwarfs.

Astonishing fact

Deneb (which means 'tail' in Arabic) is the brightest star in the constellation Cygnus (the swan). Deneb is about 60,000 times more luminous than the sun!

Studying and watching stars

Historically, stars have been important to civilizations throughout the world. They have been part of religious practices and used for celestial navigation and orientation. Many ancient astronomers believed that stars were permanently affixed to a heavenly sphere, and that they were immutable. By convention, astronomers grouped stars into constellations and used them to track the motions of the planets and the inferred position of the sun. The motion of the sun against the background stars (and the horizon) was used to create calendars, which could be used to regulate agricultural practices. The Gregorian calendar, currently used nearly everywhere in the world, is a solar calendar based on the angle of the Earth's rotational axis relative to its local star, the sun.

The concept of the constellation was known to exist during the Babylonian period. Ancient sky watchers imagined that prominent arrangements of stars formed patterns, and they associated these with particular aspects of nature or their myths. Twelve of these formations lay along the band of the ecliptic and these became the basis of astrology. Many of the more prominent individual stars were also given names, particularly with Arabic or Latin designations.

Astonishing fact

Stars have their own gravity fields, which keep them close to each other. The best example is the globular cluster, which contains millions of stars tightly held by gravity.

STARS

As well as certain constellations and the sun itself, stars as a whole have their own myths. To the Ancient Greeks, some stars represented various important deities, from which the names of the planets Mercury, Venus, Mars, Jupiter and Saturn were taken. (Uranus and Neptune were also Greek and Roman gods, but neither planet was known because of their low brightness. Their names were assigned by later astronomers).

Stars can be observed using many different tools. There are hundreds of different telescopes. There are even probes that help with the job. Probes are large mechanical devices that are used to find things in space. Some radios are tuned all day to pick up a star's movement using radio waves. Even huge telescopes cannot view all stars because some are too far away. Only strong radio waves can detect these stars.

Stellar astronomy is about the study of birth, evolution and finally death of stars. It is an immensely huge subject and occupies a large portion of the main branch of astronomy.

Some brightest stars

Sirius

Procyon is the eighth brightest star night sky. It is a yellow-white star and at 11.4 light years, one of the closer stars to Earth.

Sirius

Sirius, also known as the **Dog Star**, is the brightest star in the sky. Its name comes from the Greek word for 'scorching'. It is in the constellation Canis Major (The Great Dog). Sirius is a main sequence star that is about 70 times more luminous than the sun. It is about 8.6 light-years from Earth.

Canopus

Named either for an ancient city in northern Egypt or the helmsman for Menelaus, Canopus is the second brightest star in the sky. It is the brightest star in the southern constellation of Carina and Argo Navis.

Rigil Kentaurus

Rigel Kentaurus, also known as Alpha Centauri, is the third brightest star in the sky. Its name literally means foot of the centaur. It is actually a triple star system made up of Alpha Centauri A, Alpha Centauri B, and Alpha Centauri C (also known as Proxima Centauri because it is the closet star to Earth at 4.3 light years). Rigel Kentaurus is located in the constellation Centaurus.

Rigil kentaurus

STARS

Arcturus

Arcturus is the brightest star in the constellation Bootes, which is one of the oldest constellations in the night sky. It is the fourth brightest star in the entire sky. Arcturus means bear guard, as it overlooks the constellation Ursa Major. It is an orange giant with a diameter about 10 times that of the sun and a luminosity about 100 times that of the sun. At about 34 light-years, Arcturus is one of the nearest giant stars. Arcturus is located in the constellation Bootes.

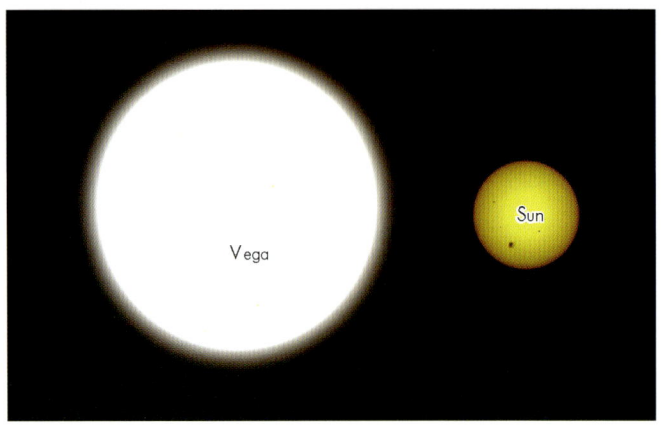

Vega

Vega is the fifth brightest star in the sky. Its name comes from Arabic meaning 'swooping eagle'. Vega is about 25 light-years from Earth. It is three times the size of the sun and 50 times as luminous. Vega is located in the constellation Lyra.

Capella

The sixth brightest star in the sky, Capella's name comes from Latin meaning little she-goat. Capella is a yellow giant star, like our own sun, but much larger. It is part of a binary star system with a red giant star. The two orbit around each other once every 104 days. Capella is approximately 41 light-years from Earth. Capella is in the constellation Auriga.

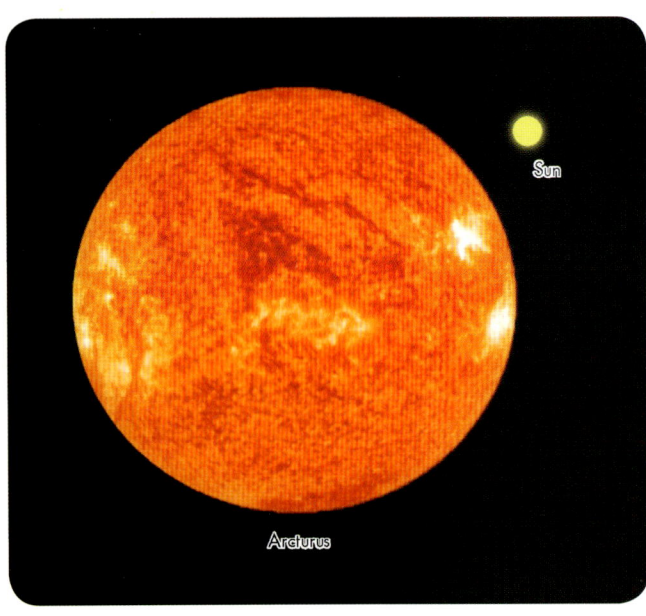

Mira (Omicron Ceti) is a well-known variable red giant star in the constellation called Cetus. It was discovered in 1596 by David Fabricus, an amateur Dutch astronomer.

Test Your MEMORY

1. What are stars?

2. Write briefly about the evolution of stars.

3. What are stars made of?

4. Write about two characteristics of stars.

5. Write about the various types of stars.

6. Why do stars twinkle?

7. How does a star look bright?

8. Write about the colour of stars.

9. How are stars named?

10. How are stars distributed in the Universe?

11. How are stars classified?

12. How can stars be studied?

Index

A
alpha 21
Alpha Centauri A 17, 29
Arcturus 30
astronomers 3, 10, 12, 13, 16, 20, 21, 23, 25, 26, 27, 28
Auriga 30

B
beta 21
binary star 7, 15, 30
Bootes 30

C
Canis Major 29
Canopus 29
Capella 30
Carina and Argo Navis 29
clusters 22
constellations 3, 5, 6, 21, 23, 25, 26, 27, 28, 30

G
galaxies 4, 13, 23
gamma 21
gas 4, 6, 7, 23

H
helium 5, 7, 8, 9, 10, 13, 24, 26
Hertzsprung-Russell (H-R) diagram 26

H
hydrogen 5, 7, 8, 9, 10, 13, 16, 24, 26

I
International Astronomical Union (IAU) 21

K
kelvin scale 12

L
luminosity 11, 12, 13, 25, 26, 30
Lyra 30

M
magnitude 11
main sequence star 13, 24, 25, 26, 29
Milky Way 6, 10, 14, 22

N
neutron star 8, 16
nucleus 5

O
Orion 6, 21
Orion Nebula 6

P
plasma 4, 11
proto-star 7
Proxima Centauri 29

R
radiation 4
red dwarf stars 16, 19
red giants 13, 18
Rigel 12, 17, 29
Rigel Kentaurus 29

S
Sirius 29
solar system 3, 10
stellar classification 24
stellar scintillation 18
supergiant stars 16

T
telescope 3, 8, 20, 22, 28

U
ultraviolet rays 4
Ursa Major 30

V
variable star 15
Vega 5, 30

W
white dwarf stars 14

X
x-rays 4